discard

Natural Disasters

SAFETY FIRST

Natural Disasters

Kim Etingoff

Mason Crest

Mason Crest
450 Parkway Drive, Suite D
Broomall, PA 19008
www.masoncrest.com

Printed and bound in the United States of America.

First printing
9 8 7 6 5 4 3 2 1

Series ISBN: 978-1-4222-3044-2
ISBN: 978-1-4222-3048-0
ebook ISBN: 978-1-4222-8832-0

Library of Congress Cataloging-in-Publication Data

Etingoff, Kim.
  Natural disasters / Kim Etingoff.
      pages cm. – (Safety first)
  Includes index.
  Audience: Ages 10+
  Audience: Grade 4 to 6.
  ISBN 978-1-4222-3048-0 (hardback)—ISBN 978-1-4222-3044-2 (series)—ISBN 978-1-4222-
8832-0 (ebook) 1. Natural disasters–Juvenile literature. I. Title.
  GB5019.E85 2015
  613.6'9–dc23
                                    2014003849

Contents

Introduction

No task is more important than creating safe schools for all children. It should not require an act of courage for parents to send their children to school nor for children to come to school. As adults, we must do everything reasonable to provide a school climate that is safe, secure, and welcoming—an environment where learning can flourish. The educational effectiveness and the strength of any nation is dependent upon a strong and effective educational system that empowers and prepares young people for meaningful and purposeful lives that will promote economic competitiveness, national defense, and quality of life.

Clearly adults are charged with the vital responsibility of creating a positive educational climate. However, the success of young people is also affected by their own participation. The purpose of this series of books is to articulate what young adults can do to ensure their own safety, while at the same time educating them as to the steps that educators, parents, and communities are taking to create and maintain safe schools. Each book in the series gives young people tools that will empower them as participants in this process. The result is a model where students have the information they need to work alongside parents, educators, and community leaders to tackle the safety challenges that face young people every day.

Perhaps one of the most enduring and yet underrated challenges facing young adults is bullying. Ask parents if they can remember the schoolyard bully from when they were in school, and the answers are quite revealing. Unfortunately, the situation is no better today—and new venues for bullying exist in the twenty-first-century world that never existed before. A single bully can intimidate not only a single student but an entire classroom, an entire school, and even an entire community. The problem is underscored by research from the National School Safety Center and the United States Secret Service that indicates that bullying was involved in 80 percent of school shootings over the past two decades. The title in this series that addresses this problem is a valuable and essential tool for promoting safety and stopping bullying.

Another problem that has been highlighted by the media is the threat of violence on our school campuses. In reality, research tells us that schools are the safest place for young people to be. After an incident like Columbine or Sandy Hook, however, it is difficult for the public, including students, to understand that a youngster is a hundred times more likely to be assaulted or killed at home or in the community than at school. Students cannot help but absorb the fears that are so prevalent in our society. Therefore, a frank, realistic, discussion of this topic, one that avoids hysteria and exaggeration, is essential for our young people. This series offers a title on this topic that does exactly that. It addresses questions such as: How do you deal with a gunman on the campus? Should you run, hide, or confront? We do not want to scare our children; instead, we want to empower them and reassure them as we prepare them for such a crisis. The book also covers the changing laws and school policies that are being put in place to ensure that students are even safer from the threat of violence in the school.

"Stranger danger" is another safety threat that receives a great deal of attention in the modern world. Again, the goal should be to empower rather than terrify our children. The book in this series focusing on this topic provides young readers with the essential information that will help them be "safety smart," not only at school but also between home and school, at play, and even when they are home alone.

Alcohol and drug abuse is another danger that looms over our young people. As many as 10 percent of American high school students are alcoholics. Meanwhile, when one student was asked, "Is there a drug problem in your school?" her reply was, "No, I can get all the drugs I want." A book in this series focuses on this topic, giving young readers the information they need to truly comprehend that drugs and alcohol are major threats to their safety and well-being.

From peer pressure to natural disasters, from road dangers to sports safety, the Safety First series covers a wide range of other modern concerns. Keeping children and our schools safe is not an isolated challenge. It will require all of us working together to create a climate where young people can have safe access to the educational opportunities that will promote the success of all children as they transition into becoming responsible citizens. This series is an essential tool for classrooms, libraries, guidance counselors, and community centers as they face this challenge.

Dr. Ronald Stephens
Executive Director
National School Safety Center
www.schoolsafety.us

Words to Know

engulfed: Surrounded or covered (usually by fire).
traumatic: Emotionally troubling or damaging.
drought: A period of time with little or no rain.
evacuated: Cleared of people for safety reasons.
generosity: Caring about and giving to other people in need.

Chapter One

A Real-Life Story

Natural disasters can be scary. People who live through them are often afraid for a long time after the disaster is over. For those people, sharing their stories can be really helpful.

One person shared her natural disaster story online. She wrote it on the website for the Experience Project, a place for people to share all kinds of stories.

The storyteller says, "In the summer of 2003, a huge area of British Columbia [a province in Canada] was **engulfed** in wildfires. It was a terrible, **traumatic** experience for thousands of people, residents and rescuers alike. I have never written about this before, not even in my journal, because just after it had happened I just did not want to go through all those emotions again. But now I can write about it." She continues to tell her story.

It was a hot, dry summer that came after two years of summers that were just as hot and just as dry. **Drought** had turned the forests to tinder. The grass in yards and fields was so dry that if you grabbed a handful, it turned to dust in your hand. Gardens were so dry that the wind blew them away. And meanwhile, it just kept getting hotter!

The young woman who went through this was on her way home from a trip to Vancouver. As she neared her town, she saw five planes circling in the air above her. Then she saw rescue vehicles

Wildfires can destroy huge areas of land—if they get out of control, both natural areas and human buildings are in danger.

and fire trucks parked along the side of the road. She still wasn't worried, though, even when she saw a plume of smoke rising above the trees. With all the emergency vehicles around, she figured people would have the fire under control in no time.

But the fire still wasn't under control by the next day. Instead, it kept growing. Ashes starting drifting down from the sky like snowflakes. Then the power went out. Now the young woman and her family were starting to get worried.

By the next morning, there was still no power. And then they heard the news: the entire area was being **evacuated**. The fire was moving their way, and if they didn't leave immediately, it might cut them off from help. It might even consume their house and their land. They were in danger if they didn't leave.

The young woman and her family got ready to go. The instructions on the radio told them to take only what they really needed—but with so little time to pack, it was hard to know what to bring! In the end, they brought their important papers and their suitcases full of clothes. They made sure their dog and cat were in the truck—and they set off, not knowing if they would ever see their home again.

They drove through smoke so thick they could hardly see six feet ahead of the truck. Everything seemed like a strange and scary dream. They could hear loud noises echoing through the trees, but not a single bird was singing. They passed emergency vehicles everywhere.

When they reached town, they knew they should fill up on gas. A long line of vehicles waited at the only gas station that was still working in an area that covered hundreds of miles. The fire had knocked down power lines, so other gas stations had no electricity to run their pumps. As the family drove on, they passed many cars that had run out of gas. Travelers stood by their cars, stranded, waiting for help.

At last the family reached the place where they would be staying. "The entire weekend was a nightmare," the young woman wrote. They tried to put on brave faces, but they were scared that their house was in ashes.

They registered with the Red Cross, which helps people and keeps things organized during and after a natural disaster. "Registering with the Red Cross?" the young woman thought. "I'm in a disaster area?" It just didn't seem real to her. How could it be possible? Nothing like this had ever happened to her before.

The family had hoped to be able to go home after a couple of days—but then smoke began to curl toward them over the lake where they were staying. The fire was continuing to spread. The evacuation wasn't over yet.

"At last we heard that our house was safe. What a relief! At last we were allowed to return home, after two weeks. There was still no power, but we were at least at home again. Everything was as we had left it. We had been warned not to open our fridges or freezers, just to tape them up and leave them out by the road for later pickup." Because the power had been off, the food inside had gone bad and could have made people sick.

The story wasn't over yet. "But we were only home three days . . . before we were evacuated yet again! This time we had to go south, so for the first time we got a good look at the devastation. It

A Real-Life Story

It is very difficult to fight a large wildfire. Firefighters use many different techniques, including firefighting planes that cover the area with chemicals that put out fires.

Natural Disasters

A disaster like the wildfire in British Columbia requires the cooperation of many emergency personnel to deal with it.

was unbelievable. Miles and miles of charcoal trees, and houses so thoroughly burned that there was absolutely nothing left but the foundations, not even ash piles or burnt out appliances."

This time the family went to Kamloops, a nearby city. It looked as though it were in the middle of a war. The fire was still raging out of control through the surrounding land, and smoke billowed in from all directions. The temperature was 113° Fahrenheit (45° Celsius), and it seemed as though the entire world was burning.

But people from all over were coming to help. Fire trucks from cities and towns across Canada and the United States drove down the streets. People cheered whenever they saw them. It was a good feeling to know they weren't facing this disaster alone.

A Real-Life Story

Organizations like FEMA in the United States help the victims of natural disasters rebuild their lives by giving them temporary housing like this.

14   **Natural Disasters**

At last the family was allowed to go back to their town. The fire was still roaring out of control—but it had passed by their home. Now it was busy destroying things somewhere else. In the end, it destroyed thousands of acres of forests, ranches, and farms.

The fire was over—but now the really hard part began. The family's friends and neighbors came back to find they no longer had homes. Life was different for everyone. For the next year, no one could think or talk about anything except the fire. It was always at the front of their minds.

"I was personally overwhelmed at the **generosity** of strangers," the young woman wrote. "Donations came from far and near and wide. Money, clothing, pet food, drinking water. A group of American women donated a handmade quilt for every bed lost in the fire, and these quilts were beautiful works of art. Mennonites, who do not do military service but instead help in disasters, came to help rebuild houses. . . .

"The land is still scarred and barren, but the green grass is back between the blackened trees. At last we can go to social gatherings and not talk about the fires. At last we can smell smoke without going into panic mode. But our lives are forever changed."

This woman's story gives you a glimpse at what living through a natural disaster is like. She was lucky; no one she knew was hurt, and her house was safe. Other people aren't always so lucky. But you can do a lot to be prepared. Learning about natural disasters and what to do when they happen can save lives.

Words to Know

rotating: Turning or twisting.
property: Things people own, like cars or houses.

Chapter Two

Why Are Natural Disasters Dangerous?

Natural disasters are emergencies caused by things that happen in nature. They cause a lot of damage and can kill or injure lots of people.

TYPES OF NATURAL DISASTERS

There are many kinds of natural disasters. Most places on Earth are in danger of some kind of natural disaster. But most places aren't in danger of all of them.

FEMA—the Federal Emergency Management Agency—lists several kinds of natural disasters. They are:

- *Drought*. When an area doesn't get rain for a long time, it's called a drought. Farm crops can die. Farm animals can die of thirst. Or they can die from hunger, because there is not enough water for the crops to grow. Even if the farm crops and animals don't die, they

You might not think of heavy snow as a natural disaster, but if it knocks out power or people are trapped in the cold, blizzards can be very dangerous to humans.

won't be as healthy as they would be with normal amounts of rain. People in the drought area must watch how much water they use. Just about any place on Earth can go through a drought.

- *Earthquakes.* Earth is made up of underground plates of rock. Sometimes those rocks shift. When this happens, it's called an earthquake. Places above where two plates come together are at the most risk for earthquakes. Earthquakes can be tiny and barely felt, or they can be huge and cause a lot of damage.
- *Extreme heat.* Temperatures that stay really hot for a long time count as a natural disaster. Extreme heat is dangerous for people and animals.
- *Floods.* Floods are the most common natural disaster. They can happen just about any-where in the world. Rivers and streams flood when there is too much rain. Melting snow and ice can also cause floods. Flash floods are particularly dangerous. Flash floods happen very suddenly and often without warning. They can come roaring in with a big wall of water.
- *Hurricanes.* People on coasts have to be careful about hurricanes (or typhoons, as they are called in the Pacific Ocean). Hurricanes bring lots of rain, high winds, and sometimes thunderstorms and tornadoes. Even people miles away from the coast can be affected by powerful hurricanes.

Natural Disasters

- *Landslides and debris flows.* Mud, rocks, sand, and more can all fall down a slope. Landslides can pick up big rocks, trees, and even objects like houses and cars. They often happen after heavy rains.
- *Thunderstorms and lightning.* Thunderstorms can produce some pretty dangerous weather—hail, heavy rain, high winds, and lightning. Lightning can strike people and start fires.
- *Tornadoes.* Tornadoes are **rotating** funnel clouds that come down from the clouds of a storm. The winds in a tornado can move faster than three hundred miles an hour! Tornadoes occur around the world, although the United States sees the most tornadoes every year.
- *Tsunamis.* Tsunamis happen when an earthquake occurs under the ocean. The earthquake causes a huge wave that travels out in all directions. If the wave hits the shore, it can cause much death and destruction.
- *Volcanoes.* Volcanoes are mountains that spill out hot lava from inside the earth. Volcano eruptions can spray into the air, or they can spill slowly down the sides. In either case, hot lava is very dangerous. Areas within twenty miles of an active volcano face the most danger.
- *Wildfires.* Areas that have a lot of woods are in danger of wildfires. Wildfires often happen when it has been dry. Lightning is usually to blame for wildfires, but humans sometimes start them by accident, for example, by not putting out a campfire or throwing away lit cigarettes. Sometimes they're started on purpose.
- *Winter storms and extreme cold.* Extreme winter weather, like blizzards and ice storms, can knock out power and heat and make roads impossible to use. Extreme cold is also dangerous for people without protection.

HOW COMMON ARE THEY?

Natural disasters aren't something that happen to you every day. But many people around the world will experience some kind of natural disaster. They probably won't see a really extreme disaster, though. Those are fairly rare.

In 2012 there were 905 natural disasters. Some, like earthquakes and tornadoes, were very destructive. Others, like severe storms or heat waves, did not cause as much damage.

Between 2000 and 2012, natural disasters affected 2.9 billion people around the world!

INJURIES AND DEATH

Probably the most obvious dangers from natural disasters are injury and death. All natural disasters can hurt people.

People get hurt in a lot of different ways during natural disasters. They can drown if there are floods. Sometimes falling objects hurt people, especially in tornadoes, hurricanes, and other storms with a lot of wind. Extreme temperatures—hot or cold—can also make people sick, especially if they are very young or very old.

Why Are Natural Disasters Dangerous?

19

Tornadoes can cause lots of property damage. This house had its whole roof torn off and carried away by the intense winds!

Natural Disasters

Where Natural Disasters Happen

Natural disasters can happen anywhere. The type of natural disaster that happens in an area depends on the climate, whether the area is on the ocean, and other geographic features. For example, a tropical town by the ocean could see a tsunami. But it probably won't see ice storms. Some countries are safer than others. In the last ten years or so, Haiti, Indonesia, Myanmar, China, Pakistan, India, Russia, Sri Lanka, Iran, and Japan have suffered the worst natural disasters. Many of those countries are poor and didn't have enough safeguards against natural disasters. Buildings in such countries are often not very sturdy, and they can easily crumble and fall during natural disasters.

Though many people experience natural disasters, far fewer are killed in them. From 2000 to 2012, 1.1 million people were killed in natural disasters. That number may seem like a lot. And each one of those deaths was a tragedy.

But think about how many people there are in the world. There are over 7 billion people. If you do the math, that represents less than .0002 percent of the world's population today—a very small percentage!

PROPERTY DAMAGE

You are much more likely to have to deal with **property** damage than being injured from a natural disaster. Natural disasters usually affect a big area. They don't just affect one family or one street. They affect a whole town. Or a whole city. Or a whole region!

In the affected area, a natural disaster can destroy a lot of buildings. Businesses, schools, homes, and more are damaged or destroyed. So are pipes that carry water and gas.

In the twelve years between 2000 and 2012, natural disasters caused a huge amount of damage. In terms of money, they caused a total of $1.7 trillion worth of damage worldwide.

Floods are the most expensive kind of natural disaster. Remember, floods can happen because of other things, like hurricanes and tornadoes. People need water to survive, but too much all at once is dangerous. Flooding damages homes and businesses. Floods carry away cars and whole buildings. Floodwater can damage roads. They're effects can be felt for a long time.

SCHOOLS

Natural disasters get in the way of school. When a hurricane is bearing down on a town, young people aren't going to be going to school! Hopefully, they'll be with their families, making their homes safe or evacuating.

And after natural disasters, people aren't thinking about school. They're thinking about rebuilding homes and businesses. The school building may even be destroyed or damaged.

If the natural disaster was really bad, young people may not be able to go to school for quite a

Natural disasters are not just dangerous because of the damage they cause right away. People must spend a long time on putting their lives back together.

while. The community has to find a place to build a new school or somewhere students can have class until a new one can be built. The school district has to figure out how to get students to school, too. The roads may be unusable. Buses may not be an option for a while.

Natural disasters cause big gaps in education. Instead of learning in school, young people are picking up the pieces after a disaster!

Florida is a state that is well prepared for natural disasters. Hurricanes pass over Florida every year. Schools in Florida are ready to teach students even when hurricanes get in the way.

After Hurricane Ivan in 2004, for example, staff from one Florida school district sent out lessons to all its students. They sent out lessons in the newspaper. The staff made sure families who didn't normally get the newspaper got the lessons.

Every lesson contained material students would have normally learned in school. They also had tips for parents to help teach their kids. So even though students weren't in school, the school tried to make sure they were still learning.

FEAR

Natural disasters can be very scary. Even though someone who has never been through a natural disaster can fear them, those who experienced the disasters firsthand can be especially afraid.

Natural Disasters

Nuta, a girl from Thailand who lived through a tsunami, described how she felt afterward to the organization Save the Children.

"There were many organizations that came in to help. But I cannot erase those old pictures of my friends. I cannot tell exactly how I feel ... my close friend died.

"When I went back to class. I was still afraid because I did not know if [the] tsunami would happen again. Some children in the class would cry and the teacher had to rush in. We were afraid even of strangers.

"There were fewer children in the classroom. Around forty-seven people in the village died. People may think that forty-seven was a small number, but I thought that it was a lot because there were not many people in my village. We all knew one another.

"It took about five to six months for the students to feel better. But I don't think that it will ever be the same. I still can't accept the fact that my friend has died."

A little fear is a good thing. People who are scared of natural disasters are more likely to try to stay safe from them. They will pay attention to evacuations and leave their homes if told to. They will have plans in place for if a natural disaster even happens.

Fear is totally normal. But too much fear gets in the way of life. You can't let your fear of natural disasters keep you from doing things you like to do. For example, if you're too scared to leave your house anymore, life won't be very fun!

Fear makes it harder to live. School gets harder, because it's harder to concentrate or care about what's going on. Fearful young people might stay away from friends or be really annoyed all the time. They might even become violent because of their feelings. Many people need help dealing with their fears.

When someone goes through a natural disaster, she might end up with post-traumatic stress disorder (PTSD). PTSD is an extreme reaction to bad situations. It is a mental illness that happens to people who have seen really scary things. Veterans of wars often have PTSD. Someone who sees his community destroyed from an earthquake or hurricane could also end up with PTSD.

People with PTSD feel scared even when they're not in danger. They sometimes relive the scary event. Often, their hearts race, and they breathe hard. They might be angry all the time. Sleeping, eating, concentrating, and doing other normal things are more difficult.

Not everyone who goes through a natural disaster develops PTSD. Luckily, people with PTSD can get help. They need to talk to doctors and counselors, who will know how to help them.

There is a lot you can do to prepare for a natural disaster. And many people are on hand to help you in case a natural disaster strikes.

Why Are Natural Disasters Dangerous?

Words to Know

technologies: Tools and ways of doing things that people have invented.
reduction: Lessening or bringing down the amount of something.
preventive measures: Steps people take to keep something bad from happening.

Chapter Three

Staying Safe and Being Prepared

Natural disasters are a part of life. Earthquakes, hailstorms, landslides, and other natural disasters will happen whether we like it or not.

However, we can do a lot to be more prepared for natural disasters. New **technologies** have made people much safer from natural disasters. And the future looks even safer.

TEACHING PEOPLE ABOUT NATURAL DISASTERS

The most important thing that helps people live through natural disasters is knowledge! If you don't know what a natural disaster is, you can't really prepare for it. Or know what to do when it's happening.

The organization Save the Children involves young people in teaching others about natural disasters. Young people everywhere are worried about natural disasters. They want to be prepared to face them. And they want to teach adults!

Save the Children has a program called Disaster Risk **Reduction** (DRR). It trains young people to teach their communities about natural disasters. Then the young people teach what to do in case of a disaster.

Young people in the DRR program learn why natural disasters happen and how to prepare for them. They learn first aid and what to do in an emergency.

Flash floods are hard to predict and can happen quickly. It's important that people know how to stay safe ahead of time.

Ple is a young girl in Thailand. She is part of the DRR program. Her community is at risk for serious floods. So she and other young people in her community have stepped up to help.

She says, "We have done a community map identifying where the risks and safe areas are. Our community map also identifies which families have children and elders, and how we can help them when a disaster strikes.

"During training, we played a game about how we needed to work together to prevent a land-slide to get into our village.

"Everyone sat on a chair but left one chair empty. [The empty chair represented a household that could not help themselves in disasters.] A person playing a role of a landslide tried to get that empty chair from the village. So everyone had to rotate to sit on the empty chair and prevent the landslide from taking any empty chair from us. . . . We will have an actual emergency drill soon.

"It is best to inform people in advance where the safe areas are. We can use the community radio broadcast to inform people where those areas are—where people can run to and stay away from the floods. It is better to let them know in advance.

"We should also tell them what they should prepare to pack. As someone who received train-ings, I want to pass on my knowledge to other people in my community. Also, when they learn about disasters and that they are partly caused by humans, we will find **preventive measures** together so that they can protect themselves and others when there is a disaster."

Natural Disasters

Earthquake Simulation Script

Sometimes it helps to imagine what a natural disaster might be like. You'll be better prepared if you know what to expect. The following script is part of the Hands-on Earthquake Learning Package from a group called the Environmental Volunteers, Inc. A teacher is supposed to read the script, so the students have an idea of what living through an earthquake might feel like.

Imagine that you hear a low, rumbling, roaring sound. The noise builds, getting louder and louder, for a few seconds. Then, Wham! There's a terrific jolt. You feel like someone suddenly slammed on the brakes in the car, or like a truck just rammed into the side of the building.

The floor seems to be moving beneath you. It's hard to stand up, or even stay in your seat. If you do stand up, you might feel like you're riding a raft down a fast river. When you walk, it's like trying to walk on a trampoline or a waterbed. You hear someone say, "Earthquake! Drop, Cover, and Hold!"

I want all of you at your desks to take cover as quickly and quietly as you can, right now. Please listen very carefully.

The shaking and commotion may last about 60 seconds or a little longer. We'll have our timer count off the seconds for as long as this earthquake lasts.

The building is creaking and rattling. Books are falling from the bookcase. Hanging lamps and plants are swaying. Suddenly a pot falls to the floor and smashes, and the plant spills. A window pane just shattered, and glass is falling to the floor. The table is sliding, too.

Be sure to stay in the drop, cover, and hold position under your desk. If your desk is moving, grab the legs and move with it.

You hear noises outside. Dogs are barking. Cats are meowing. A baby is crying. People are shouting and screaming. The shaking is making church bells ring. You hear crashing sounds, from brick chimneys and other loose parts of the building falling to the ground. Trees outside are swaying and scraping against the walls.

Inside the room, pictures are moving on their nails. Oh! That one just fell off the wall and crashed to the floor. The desk drawers are sliding open. The lights begin to flicker on and off … they just went out! Now the door swings back and forth on its hinges. Bang! It slams shut.

There's silence now. Just as suddenly as the noise and shaking began, the room grows quiet.

Please, everyone, get back in your seats. It is important to remain very quiet and wait for instructions. When it is safe to leave the building, I am going to lead you outside to an open space.

Stay together, and be ready to take cover again at any moment, because the shaking may start again. Sometimes other quakes, called aftershocks, occur after the damaging earthquake has stopped.

In the past, floods have made roads and bridges unusable where Ple lives. Every year, she and her classmates can't go to school for a few days because of the floods. But Ple knows the flooding could be much worse. She wants to make sure people are prepared and safe.

Modern technology lets us closely track hurricanes from space, predicting when and where they are likely to strike.

28 **Natural Disasters**

When you know a hurricane is coming, it's important to prepare by gathering supplies and boarding up the building in which you're taking shelter.

And she thinks young people are key. "Adults may have a bigger role [in DRR] than the children," she says. "However, the children can help educate and improve the understanding of those who may not yet know about this issue.

"Educating adults can be a role of the children. For some adults, because they have experienced disasters, they can also help children when a disaster happens. It's like we have different kind of knowledge to share."

Ple and others like her know education can save lives. People who are prepared for natural disasters survive!

PREPARING FOR NATURAL DISASTERS

Scientists have gotten pretty good at predicting many of the biggest natural disasters. For example, we now know when hurricanes are coming days before they hit land. Hurricanes form over the ocean. Meteorologists, scientists who study the weather, track them and predict where they will go. These scientists can warn people living in the hurricane's path.

When people know a hurricane is coming ahead of time, they can get ready. They can board up windows. Some towns and cities will even evacuate people, if they know the hurricane is going to be especially dangerous.

Other natural disasters are a little harder to predict. Earthquakes happen without warning. Scientists can't really tell exactly when and where one will strike.

After a natural disaster, communities will often come together to help each other get through the tough period of rebuilding.

People need to always be prepared for earthquakes. Many cities in earthquake zones have laws about how to construct buildings. Buildings must be extra strong, so they can withstand an earthquake. This saves money and prevents injuries in an earthquake.

Other natural disasters fall between having lots of warning and no warning at all. Tornadoes are one example. Meteorologists can often tell if a storm is likely to produce a tornado. And they know when and where tornadoes are most common, so they're on the lookout for them. But scientists still can't tell exactly when or where a tornado will strike. They issue tornado watches for an area if there are storms that could produce them. A tornado warning is issued if a tornado is spotted. People know to seek shelter immediately when they hear a tornado warning.

PREVENTING NATURAL DISASTERS

A few natural disasters can actually be prevented. These are disasters that happen because of things people have done.

Take landslides. Landslides happen when rock and dirt are washed down a slope, like a mountainside. Landslides happen naturally. But they happen a lot more because of people.

When people cut down trees and remove bushes and other plants on hillsides and mountainsides, landslides happen more often. The trees and plants were holding onto the dirt with their roots. They were keeping rocks and dirt from washing away.

Natural Disasters and Climate Change

Many scientists argue that we will be experience more and more natural disasters as time goes on because of climate change. Climate change happens because things we use, like vehicles, and manufacturing processes put greenhouse gases, like carbon dioxide, into the air. These gases trap heat, making Earth warmer. One of the effects of climate change is more extreme storms and strange weather patterns. Scientists believe droughts, hurricanes, severe thunderstorms, and more will happen more often.

When those trees and other plants are taken out, nothing is left to hold on to the dirt and rock. So when a lot of rain comes along, it—along with the soil—washes right down the slope.

Another preventable natural disaster is wildfire. Fires do happen naturally, such as when lightning strikes somewhere that is really dry. And fires are actually good for nature; they help keep forests healthy! But people set some wildfires. Someone accidentally starts a fire in a dry area. Then the fire gets out of control. In a few cases, a person starts a fire on purpose. If people didn't set fires, there would be fewer wildfires that destroy homes and lives.

HELPING AFTER A NATURAL DISASTER

There will always be natural disasters. It's just part of our world. Many communities who are prepared for disasters also have plans for what happens after. People will need help, and communities are ready to give that help.

Many organizations exist to help people in need. The Red Cross is one. Workers with the Red Cross bring needed supplies, like bottled water and food. They help people reunite with their families and find places to live if their homes have been destroyed. The Red Cross slowly helps communities get back to normal.

In the United States, FEMA helps people, too. FEMA sends people into the area to do search and rescues for missing people. It also brings in needed supplies and helps communities rebuild. Where homes can no longer be lived in, they provide temporary housing. Around the world, the United Nations steps into help after a natural disaster. Without organizations like these, rebuilding would take a lot longer.

Words to Know

generators: Machines that make energy to power lights and electronics when the power goes out.

bacteria: Small creatures living all around us. Some bacteria can make us very sick. Bacteria are often called "germs."

therapist: Someone who is trained to talk with you about your problems and to help you feel better.

recovery: The rebuilding done after a disaster.

Chapter Four

What Can You Do to Stay Safe?

One of the scariest things about natural disasters is the feeling that you can't do anything about them. They'll happen anyway, right? How can you avoid them?

You can't stop natural disasters from happening. But you can stay out of their way if you know what to do. And you can help people rebuild their lives after natural disasters. People and communities are stronger than disasters!

LEARN ABOUT NATURAL DISASTERS

You have to know what a natural disaster is to protect yourself! Learning about natural disasters saves lives. Ismael's story helps show how important knowing about natural disasters is.

Ismael is a young person living in Thailand. In 2004, he, some classmates, and a teacher were at school rehearsing for a play. They looked out the window and saw the ocean was gone!

They went outside to look around. And then the tsunami hit. A huge wave roared in and washed everything away.

Ismael survived. Sadly, most of the other people who had been rehearsing for the play didn't.

Ismael and his friends hadn't known what a tsunami was. Far out in the ocean, an earthquake

In a place like Thailand where tsunamis are a risk, it's important that people know how to respond to such a disaster. These signs tell people what to do in both English and the Thai language.

Natural Disasters

Tsunamis are huge waves that travel quickly across the ocean. Since they strike so quickly, it is very difficult to prepare for them.

caused a giant wave to form. When the ocean disappeared, all of the water drew back from the shore into that big wave. Then the wave reached the shore and destroyed everything. If they had known, Ismael and the others could have run away from the shore.

After the tsunami, people in the village were scared. What if it happened again? Students didn't want to go to school and leave their families. Loud bangs sent people into a panic. No one would go near the ocean.

Ismael's story also shows how to heal from a natural disaster. The people of Ismael's village had to go on with their lives.

A local organization, along with Save the Children, wanted to help people heal. The leaders of the groups told people to focus on the positive. There were still many people alive. And they could rebuild the village.

Young people played a big part in rebuilding. They built a new garden where the schoolyard

A disaster kit should include not only food and water, but ways to stay warm and signal for help. You might be on your own without power for a while.

Natural Disasters

used to be. They also created a play about tsunamis. The play taught people what tsunamis were and what to do about them. Ismael was part of the play. The play helped him feel better about what happened, because he was helping other people learn.

Then Ismael and other young people came up with a new play. They wanted to teach very young children about tsunamis. They created a puppet play called *The Alert Rabbit*. They also turned the play into a children's book. The play and the book have taught many little kids about the dangers of tsunamis.

Ismael told Save the Children he felt better after the tsunami by working to help others learn about natural disasters. "What make[s] me feel better are activities that I have done with the youth group," he said. "I feel that I can give my friends knowledge by educating them about disasters." Ismael and others like him use teaching as a way to help their communities.

BE PREPARED

You and your family should have an emergency plan in case of a natural disaster. First, figure out what natural disasters could affect your area. You don't have to worry about an ice storm if you live where it never gets cold. And you don't have to worry about flooding on top of a hill, or a tsunami if you live hundreds of miles from the ocean.

Once you figure out which natural disasters could happen, plan! Ask yourself where you would go in case of a natural disaster. For example, if there was a tornado warning, you could go to your basement, where you're safer.

Find out if there are evacuation routes in your town. Or shelters to go to in case of a disaster. Check with your neighbors to see if they have places to go in case of emergencies. Talk to your family about how you will find each other if you're separated in an emergency.

Your school should also have an emergency plan. Ask your teacher or other adult at school what that plan is, if they haven't already told you. Your school should have a plan to keep students safe. There should also be a plan to get in touch with students' families.

Another way to prepare for a natural disaster is to build a kit. A disaster kit has all the things you need to live on for three days.

Put your kit together before a natural disaster happens. You don't want to be scrambling around at the last minute, trying to find the things you need. Make sure to keep everything together. A large plastic container is a good storage option. Whatever you keep it in, make sure it's waterproof.

EVACUATE!

Before some natural disasters, people may be asked to evacuate. Local and state governments want to protect people, so they ask them to leave when they know something like a wildfire is coming.

Some people don't take evacuations seriously. They think their home could never be destroyed. They could never be hurt. They think the evacuation is just annoying. But evacuations are no joke. In some cases, an evacuation is a case of life and death.

Ignoring an evacuation is very, very dangerous. People are evacuated to be safe. Government

Part of being prepared for a natural disaster includes knowing more than one evacuation route ahead of time, just in case one route is blocked.

Natural Disasters

Pack Your Own Disaster Kit

Here are the things your kit should have:

- Three gallons of water per person
- Three-day supply of food that won't go bad, like canned food—and a manual can opener
- Flashlight with extra batteries—make sure the batteries fit the flashlight
- Battery-powered radio
- First-aid kit
- Plates and utensils
- Cell phone with charger
- Any medications you or your family are taking
- Pet food and water for any pets
- Extra cash
- Important papers, such as insurance policies

officials and scientists don't know for sure just how dangerous a natural disaster is going to be. So they ask people to leave their homes and go somewhere else.

Evacuations also help those dealing with the natural disaster. For example, if you are ordered to evacuate because of a wildfire but decide not to go, you may be putting firefighters' lives in danger. If the fire reaches your home, firefighters will have to face even higher risks to rescue you and your family. And that's assuming they can reach you! Plus, they'll have to stop fighting the fire to attempt a rescue.

Maybe if you don't evacuate, you'll be OK. The hurricane or wildfire might not come near where you live. Or it might not be very strong. That's a huge risk to take, though! It's much better to be safe than sorry.

Evacuations are a big deal. You have to leave your home behind. You have to board a bus or drive somewhere else. People who evacuate are often put in a school, hotel, or sports complex far from danger.

While you're evacuated, you don't know what's going on at home. You don't know if your home and stuff are OK. But you'll know you and your family are safe, and that's the most important thing. Many of the people who are injured or killed in natural disasters did not evacuate when they were told to go.

STAYING SAFE AFTER A DISASTER

People are in danger while the wildfire is burning and the hurricane is blowing, but they're still in some danger after natural disasters, too.

After disasters strike, buildings are damaged. Water and gas pipes aren't working. People are hurt and scared.

What Can You Do to Stay Safe?

In serious emergencies, rescuers might need to use boats or helicopters to get trapped people to safety.

When a whole town is destroyed by a disaster, it's hard to know what to do—so you should make a plan in advance so you're prepared.

You should know what to do after natural disasters, not just before and during them. You don't want to survive a natural disaster just to get hurt after it's over! Here are a few tips:

- Clean up wet surfaces. Heavy rain can leave pools of water that grow mold in your home or offer mosquitoes a place to lay eggs.
- Stay away from any animals wandering outside; they could bite you.
- Don't use grills, camp stoves, or gas **generators** inside. Anything that uses gas or charcoal can produce carbon monoxide, which can kill you.
- Throw out food in your refrigerator if the power has been off for more than a few hours. It may have spoiled. When in doubt, throw it out.

What Can You Do to Stay Safe?

If you can help during or after a disaster, you should. It will take everyone's cooperation to rebuild back to where the community was before the disaster.

Natural Disasters

Shelter-in-Place

You may be asked to "shelter-in-place." That means you have to stay where you are, wherever that is. If you're at home, you have to stay at home. If you're inside the school, you have to stay in the school building. The point of shelter-in-place is to keep people safe. It might be more dangerous for people to travel outside than to just stay home.

- Drink only bottled water until you know your tap water is safe to drink. Water from the tap could have **bacteria** or chemicals in it after a disaster.
- Clean and bandage any cuts you have. Go to a doctor or hospital if you have any serious injuries.
- Talk to a **therapist** if you still feel really scared and worried long after the natural disaster is over. Therapists can help you get back to a normal life.

GIVE YOUR HELP

You hear or read about a natural disaster in the news. You see pictures of horrible destruction and homeless and crying people.

When you see the news or hear about a natural disaster, you might want to help. There are plenty of ways to help out after a natural disaster.

You can donate money. You can also donate materials. Sometimes people have lost everything they own. You can donate things like furniture, clothes, kitchen supplies, and food.

You can also volunteer. If you live near where the natural disaster happened, you can donate your time. The community affected by the disaster may need you to bring water to people. You might help out in an evacuation shelter. You might sort the supplies being donated. There is a lot to do after a disaster! Make sure you work with a team and follow orders. Otherwise, you might get in workers' way and cause trouble more than help.

Some people donate blood. If you are over sixteen or seventeen (depending on your state), you can give blood. After big natural disasters, many people may be injured. Some of them have lost a lot of blood. Donating blood is a way to save lives.

After a disaster, the news usually tells you who is organizing the **recovery**. That's the organization you should donate to. Often, it is the Red Cross, UNICEF (the United Nations Children's Fund), or the Salvation Army. Local organizations also often collect donations.

If you donate money or things, make sure it's going to the right people. Don't give to someone who just knocks on your door and is part of an organization you've never heard of.

Unfortunately, every once in a while, someone sets up a fake organization to steal money from people. Do your research. Make sure the organization you're donating to really exists.

Natural disasters can be terrible, but if everyone in a community is prepared and works together, things can return to normal before too long.

Natural Disasters

The Best Way to Help

After a disaster, many people can't wait to help those in need. Keep in mind the people onsite best know what is needed. Although you may be anxious to collect food, blankets, and the like, that may not be what's needed most. Unless you are specifically told something is needed and have a specific place to send or deliver the goods, it's always best to send money to an organization you know can be trusted to help.

Helping other people makes you feel better about what happened. Just seeing a natural disaster on the news can make you sad. Helping those people makes their lives a little better.

If you are in a natural disaster, many people will help you, too. You'll feel better knowing there are lots of good people out there, willing to help you.

You may never be in a natural disaster. But you should still learn as much as you can about them. Even if you never have to use your knowledge, you'll feel safer just knowing you can deal with a disaster if it ever happens.

Natural disasters can happen anywhere. Be prepared, plan ahead, and take natural disasters seriously. You'll be much safer and much happier if you do!

Find Out More

ONLINE

FEMA
www.ready.gov/kids-old/know-facts

Natural Disasters, How to Help
kidshealth.org/teen/misc/natural_disaster.html#cat117

Types of Disasters
kidshealth.org/kid/watch/er/disasters.html#

Natural Disasters
www.kidskonnect.com/subjectindex/15-educational/science/92-natural-disasters.html

Natural Disasters
environment.nationalgeographic.com/environment/natural-disasters

IN BOOKS

Burnie, David. *Disasters*. New York: Scholastic, Inc., 2013.

Hollingsworth, Tamara Leigh. *Unforgettable Natural Disasters*. Huntington Beach, Calif.: Teacher Created Materials, 2013.

Langley, Andrew. *Natural Disasters: Hurricanes, Tsunamis, and Other Destructive Forces*. New York: Kingfisher, 2006.

Watts, Claire, and Trevor Day. *Natural Disasters*. New York: DK Publishing, 2012.

Index

About the Author & Consultant

Kim Etingoff lives in Boston, Massachusetts. She spends part of her time working on farms, and enjoys writing on topics related to health and nutrition.

Dr. Ronald D. Stephens currently serves as executive director of the National School Safety Center. His past experience includes service as a teacher, assistant superintendent, and school board member. Administrative experience includes serving as a chief school business officer, with responsibilities over school safety and security, and as vice president of Pepperdine University.

Dr. Stephens has conducted more than 1000 school security and safety site assessments throughout the United States. He was described by the *Denver Post* as "the nation's leading school crime prevention expert." Dr. Stephens serves as consultant and frequent speaker for school districts, law enforcement agencies and professional organizations worldwide. He is the author of numerous articles on school safety as well as the author of *School Safety: A Handbook for Violence Prevention*. His career is distinguished by military service. He is married and has three children.

Picture Credits

discard